Broadland Sketches

by David Poole of Norwich

Cetti's warbler

Wilson-Poole publishers

Acknowledgements

Libraries have always been a favourite place of mine. When I was very small and could just about see the librarian's deft handling of returned books and tickets and saw the polished floors and tidy rows of fascinatingly different books on the shelves, perhaps then began the dream to prepare my own book to add to such storehouses. Librarians are very patient, kind and helpful and therefore genuinely I extend my appreciation for their help to me: Alan Atherton at Eastern Counties Newspapers who permitted me to draw from some press photographs; the staff at St. William's Way, Thorpe Road, and the Central Library, Norwich, for research into visual and textual records.

Ted Ellis has been cheerfully encouraging from when we first met and he said, 'Hold on to the original idea'; lending me his camera to photograph him at work; authorising the use of extracts from his book, E.A. Ellis, 'The Broads'; to writing the beautiful foreword. Peter Aldous, secretary of The Broads Society, gave me valuable background information and lent me two informative documents: 'Report on Broadland', by The Nature Conservancy, 1965 and 'Broadland, Study and Plan' by The Broads Consortium, 1971.

Owen Waters' essay is all I had hoped he would write, knowing something of his unique friendships, knowledge and link within the gifted chain of local landscape painters.

John Buxton, manager of Horsey Estate loaned me a photograph album from which three of the illustrations are drawn.

Alec Cotman kindly allowed me to draw from a watercolour by F.J. Watson. Peter Seymour generously gave me four of the Edward Seago exhibition catalogues.

Charles Nicholas, lecturer in photography, Norwich School of Art, allowed me to draw from three transparencies he loaned me. Likewise, Hallam Ashley, another gifted local photographer, permitted me to draw from three of his bromides.

Woven into the text are captions used by permission of the Nature Conservancy Council.

Other men, including Mr. Timothy Colman, The Lord Lieutenant of Norfolk, James Hoseason, Eric Fowler, Robin Harrison, Michael Dixon and Alan Savory, gave me valuable advice and background information.

Above all I am grateful to my friend and publisher Don Wilson of Horning who had enough confidence in me to finance a significant part of the origination and consequently gave me 'breathing space' within which I could find the freedom to draw more effectively.

ISBN 0 9506592 0 7

Phototypeset by Hugh Wilson Typesetting, Norwich
Repro by Photomation, Norwich
Printed and bound in the United Kingdom by Page Bros (Norwich) Ltd.

Contents

Foreword

by
Doctor E.A. Ellis
(affectionately known as Ted,
naturalist,writer, photographer, T.V.
personality)

The Broadland of East Norfolk and adjacent Suffolk has a haunting beauty and unique interest for those who adventure on its waterways. Its shallow lakes, some windswept in open marsh country and others limpid and encircled by swampy fen woodlands, are in most cases connected with a network of gently tidal rivers. In summer the fringing reeds are a home of chattering warblers and at all seasons give shelter to curious and delightful birds such as the bittern, water rail and bearded tit. Waterfowl abound and the wild music of marsh birds adds to the delights of spring. The broads and marsh dykes have long been the habitat of many fascinating water plants and insects, while reeds and sedges at the waterside are mingled with resplendent wild flowers of every colour in summer. Where the rivers emerge from the jungle-like intimacy of their valleys and wander as silver threads across the flat and far-flung grazing levels towards the sea, sails of yachts catch the breeze like birds' wings, gracing the landscape where old mills loom up here and there like shadows of the past. Long ago this was a wild tract of untamed fen and estuarine floodland; for a time it became the scene of great activity when peat-diggers were excavating the basins of the broads, but thereafter it long remained almost exclusively a haunt of wild nature, reed-cutters, wildfowlers and fishermen, until its holiday attractions came to be appreciated increasingly from the mid-nineteenth century onwards.

This East Anglian wonderland of light and freedom in which Nature provides enchantment for artist, naturalist and all others who seek happiness in gentle exploration under the open sky can survive only if we all combine to cherish it in a sympathetic and responsible way.

E.A.E.
Wheatfen
Surlingham, Norfolk

As a boy I fished with worm and string for sticklebacks in the Bridgewater Canal and watched horses towing the narrow boats to and from Manchester. I chased and caught numerous catfish in sparkling brooks and learned to swim in the River Bollen. With the likes of Baldy Wilson and Handsome Hackett I adventured about the waters of Sale, Cheshire. We often travelled through a forbidding tunnel that ran from a gasometer beside Hooley Woods and under the canal and railway line to emerge in dazzling sunlight at the edge of the Mersey meadows and to a pond where we set sail on the rummest range of rafts imaginable.

Broadland is unique and such a great contrast to what I had experienced as a boy. In those peopleless times, in a quiet corner, or especially in winter it is like a paradise. It refreshes and revives me; uplifts and encourages me with its wide wild marsh and its timelessness. Beneath its skies I feel an exhilaration that sweeps me up into its being capturing my desire to be free of earth and to rise like a migrant bird and to fly high into its vastness.

I walk beside reedbeds and listen to the whispering of the wind about its ancient murmurings or feel strangely frightened when it roars rampant beneath lowering grey clouds racing within North Easterly gales ripping through trees and scourging them of rotten branches. By dykes and rivers there can be such peace. My heart has felt near to bursting at the sight of sunset overlaid with graceful sails feeding on the last breath of the breeze. Yet is is the ghostly heron, which has a trick of rising into the air with such lazy facility, that symbolises much of the wildness of the place and when aloft its large wings spread full span – how beautiful it is asail upon the wind.

Here then is literally a sketchbook, a brief but deliberate effort to capture a little of this area. Certainly much is missing: can you catch a whale with a bent pin? I am so heartily glad it is done. I have had a lot of adventure, fun and stimulus and above all I have learned more of this lovely place and present something of what I have heard and seen as a collection of drawings and jottings that I trust you will enjoy and consider worth treasuring.

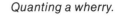

Quanting a wherry.

The quant is a stout long pole with a toe to prevent it sinking into the muddy river bottom. Wherrymen had no easy task in moving their vessels by this method in windless conditions, but with an understanding of the tides and the periodic help of even the faintest breeze, long distances could be covered as a wherryman called Walter Powley was reported as achieving when he and his mate Brown quanted from Norwich to Breydon Water.

Origins

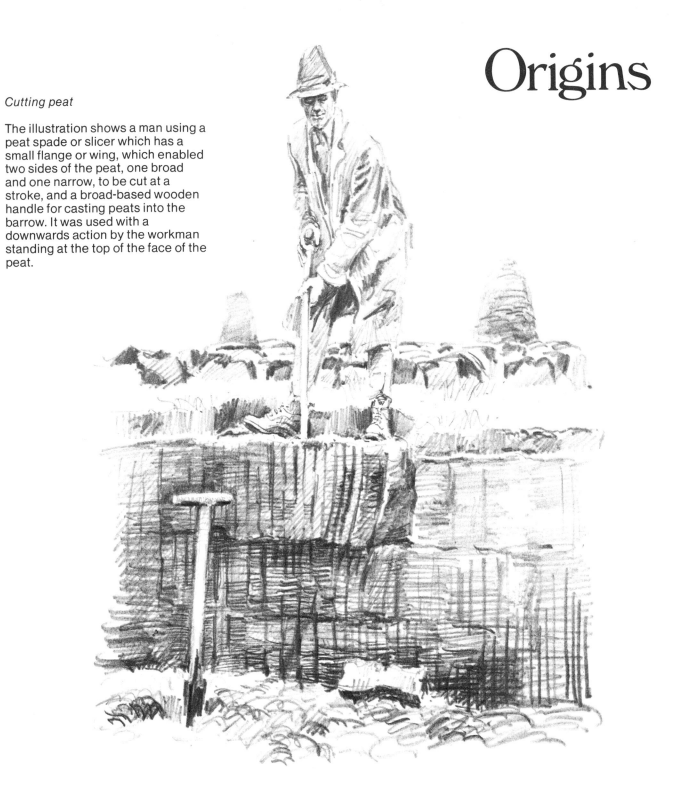

Cutting peat

The illustration shows a man using a peat spade or slicer which has a small flange or wing, which enabled two sides of the peat, one broad and one narrow, to be cut at a stroke, and a broad-based wooden handle for casting peats into the barrow. It was used with a downwards action by the workman standing at the top of the face of the peat.

The Broads are flooded pits, the result of extensive peat diggings carried out between the ninth and fourteenth centuries at a time when sea levels were four metres lower than they are today. Norfolk and Suffolk were densely populated counties during this period and peat, which when dried forms a highly combustible fuel, was in great demand for domestic heating and cooking. By the end of the fourteenth century rising sea levels caused frequent flooding of the excavations and this led to their progressive abandonment.

However, surface peat continued to be taken from shallow excavations until the beginning of this century, although this was of inferior quality. Evidence of their origin can be seen on tithe maps that show close set lines such as that of Surlingham Broad 1839, indicating a dividing up into workings. Recent in line close-set bores across broads have indicated steep-sided peat edges, islands or peninsulas of solid peat surrounded by deep lake muds.

Impervious clay separated the deep excavations from the rivers and effectively reduced lateral water seepage, as has been seen when a swimming pool at Hickling and Lound reservoirs upstream of Fritton Lake were excavated. Basic ladle and gantry removal of flood water and diversion of surface water by catch drains gave reasonable control. The waterways retained the bulk of traffic with staithes connecting rivers to isolated villages and farms. The roads were crude affairs, even with the addition of marl or chalk, being more difficult to use in bad weather.

Deep peat cutting

Great numbers of people were involved. Hard, back-breaking toil followed the heavy barrowing out of the cut peat to the drying areas. Here men were employed all summer long in cutting peat. Their spades, kept bright and sharp as razors, lasted only two seasons.

Shallow peat cutting

The peats can be seen deposited near the cutter and also in the middle distance stacked ready for collection and transport.

South Walsham records reveal that in the second half of the fourteenth century 200,000 turves or peats yielded an income of £7.00 a year. A turf or peat is approximately one quarter of a cubic foot.

St. Benet's, the ruined gateway and ▷
windmill

The monks found the 'holm' or partial island in the Bure valley ideally suited to their needs for isolation, although they provided care for the sick and could be reached via causeway or river.

In 1287 John of Oxnead, monk of St. Benet's, described a dreadful breaching of the sand dunes by Horsey through which the sea poured so quickly that many of the 180 persons drowned were still in their beds.

Consequently, the banks and marsh boundaries of the site were built up to offset the flooding menace. It is interesting to note that from the dredging of dykes it is evident that at one time an estuary existed right up to the high ground of St. Benet's.

Background

Winter St. Benedict's Abbey

Wherries loading by mill

The use of the waterways hereabouts is an ancient one, it being considered probable that the Romans used barges to transport supplies and stone for the provision and building of towns like Venta Icenorum (Caistor St Edmund, by Norwich).

Wherries are a local craft, with a single great sail attached to a gaff, that can be raised up a stout pine mast counterbalanced delicately for ease of lowering for bridge negotiation. The foot of the sail is free and only attached to sheet blocks, and these in turn to a horse mounted over the cabin or cosy. The hulls are clinker built of two inch oak overlapping strakes. Smaller wherries could use the cuts or staithes that connected villages and mills etc to the rivers; larger vessels the cuts and canals like Haddiscoe and Dilham. These vessels were seen in full use from the nineteenth to the early twentieth century plying from the sheltered Yarmouth Roads to all accessible points inland.

Improved roads and the introduction of the more reliable railways spelt their doom and sadly they declined. Only the wherry Albion remains of the traders. Her companions have been converted or purpose-built as pleasure wherries like the Olive, or have been sunk as the three by the floating observatory on Ranworth Broad.

Harry Thain born 6th July, 1902
West Somerton

Harry recalls repair sheds at the side of the village staithe and says there are sunken wherries on the way to Martham visible at low tide. He helped to repair the breeches in the sea wall during the flooding in 1953. He saw the wherry at its best, trading to and from his village. A riverman who into his seventies retains that merry sparkle of delight in his eyes as he recollects the bright memories of eelcatching, wildfowling, engineering and other diverse pursuits. As an engineer he worked on trawlers and on torpedo boats during the war.

A.D. 850 to the Norman Conquest in 1066, the late Saxon or Viking Age saw the most momentous changes in broadland. For during these two centuries many existing villages were established as well as some which disappeared in the Middle Ages, such as Bradeston by Brundall whose inhabitants were struck with the Black Death. Names like Hemsby, Filby, Mautby, Clippesby and Billockby sprung from the concentrated settlement of the mainly Danish invaders in the area known as Flegg Hundreds. 'Northwic' as described on early tenth-century coins was the result of the drawing together of scattered villages and was the crude stuff from which the more deliberate Normans later fashioned Norwich.

The large population grazed sheep and caused the production of salt in large quantities for the annual curing of the slaughtered livestock for which there was no winter feed. The strange naming of the subdivided marshes about Yarmouth is due to the allotment to villages like Postwick twelve miles inland.

Some of the best and most varied fenland systems in Britain are found in Broadland; the region still possesses large blocks of unreclaimed fen and with natural variations in peat depth, moisture levels and fertility, a unique range of plant communities has developed supporting such unusual species as Fen Orchid, Cowbane, Crested Buckler Fen, and Wintergreen. The

Friesian resting with calf

Geese over Hickling

beautiful Swallowtail butterfly is now restricted to those fens where the food plant for the caterpillar, Mike Parsley, still thrives. The extensive open reed and sedge beds provide the habitat for the Marsh Harrier and Bittern and Bearded Tit while the fen invaded by bushes has become the haunt of the Cetti's Warbler (see title page), a species which is spreading throughout the area in contrast to

the Bittern which is sadly declining. Dyke systems were essential for the removal of harvested crops such as sedge and reed used in thatching, marsh hay, much of which was sent to London as fodder for cab horses, and marsh litter for use as cattle bedding. This regular cropping of the fenlands prevented the natural development of woodland and so maintained suitable conditions for wetland plants and animals.

Derelict wherries (after F.J. Watson in possession of Alec Cotman)

A corner of Ludham village from the churchyard

Cattle by gate

With the need to grow more food from our own resources, agricultural policy now fosters the conversion of grazing marsh to arable cultivation. Wildfowl and geese are being displaced from their traditional feedings grounds; while deepening of dykes or in some cases their piping and in-filling substantially reduces their biological richness causing loss of insect and plant life.

There have been catastrophic changes in the wildlife of the Broads and their associated waterways and it is only the more isolated broads that still contain any semblance of their former ecological wealth. Great numbers of waterfowl which used to nest and feed on the broads have declined equally dramatically as plantlife, leaving only a few species most of which are dependant on man, either directly or indirectly, for food, such as coot, moorhen and cross bred ducks. The loss of aquatic plants has had an effect on insect and fish populations.

The illustration of the large pool by the maltings is interesting for the same area has now been reduced by 'die-back' of open water to staithe width.

Boatshed and geese at Horsey Mere

Wherries at Vauxhall Railway Station

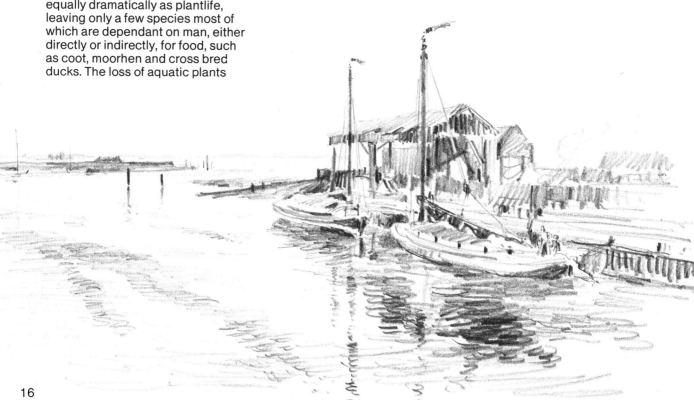

Old Maltings at Ranworth

The last of the Herring Drifters, the 'Lydia Eve', left for the Greenwich Maritime Museum late last year during the Tall Ships Race. There had been a time when you could have walked across the Yare downriver of Haven Bridge, Yarmouth across the decks of hundreds of such Drifters. Yarmouth, built from a sandbar on a pattern of drying fishing nets laid between huts that developed into narrowly spaced rows of tenements, is full of interest both historical and present day.

Yarmouth inshore fishing boat

17

Dr Ted Ellis studying a slide specimen

Undoubtedly the most dramatic effect on the broadland waterways has been the loss of aquatic plants and the clear water in which they grew. Naturalists first noticed that changes were occurring at Barton Broad in the late 1930's. However, it was not until the late 1950's that similar changes were observed in the Bure Broads. The Yare Broads soon followed leaving only Hickling Broad and Horsey Mere apparently intact. But not for long, for by 1969 similar changes were observed and by the early 1970's they too had become green, turbid and virtually devoid of water weeds. The food chain supporting insects, fish and waterfowl was thus broken with widespread repurcussions.

Stracey Arms in winter (after a painting by Edward Seago)

This mill was restored by the joint efforts of The Norfolk Windmills Trust and The National Conservation Corps in 1976.

People and Crafts

Wheelwright having dropped the iron rim over the wheel pours water on the expanded metal and clouds of steam rise as the wheel is gripped by the contracting hoop.

'Old' Sam Warnes

Sam has lived a varied and interesting life in and around Martham for sixty years. He has worked with Harry Thain and Tosh Sadler of West Somerton about the rivers and marshes and seems to be a jack-of-all-trades: reedcutting, dyke drawing, stacking and thatching, deep sea fishing on drifters, hedging and ditching but most fondly, dealing. At present he is helping to set up a museum at Church Farm, Martham. He said with a smile that he would like to see a book written about 'Tricks o' the trade', a typical recollection being how a butcher in the evening asked a customer to hold a candle and look hard at the scales and as he did so the wily butcher craftily nudged the meat in his own favour.

Norman Webb, eelcatcher and wildfowler

Norman was the most reluctant of the persons I met with. He lives with his brother in a riverside village and laughingly remarks that I always catch him peeling potatoes or cutting meat for the pot when I call. I thought of a fine painting of Vermeer as I watched Norman in a similar domestic situation. Because of his hesitation to be drawn I sketched only briefly. Eventually there came a day when, calling on the off chance, I found him slightly worried by a sore, rheumaticky leg and this enabled me to persuade him to sit down and rest it for a few minutes whilst I quickly drew his head. This small drawing is as prized as any other in the book. Their living room is full of the atmosphere of my boyhood: black iron fireplace, homely careless clutter and years of dust. I cannot resist the comparison with the decor of a modern, sterile 'frightened to be lived in' room.

Reedcutter by Horsey Mere bundling reed in the traditional manner

The widespread abandonment of traditional management practices such as sedge harvesting and litter cutting has allowed much open fen to develop into sallow scrub and dense jungle like alder woodland. The development of special machines ensure some continuation of reed cutting. However, as these machines require large areas of level reedbed to work efficiently, their use is limited.

An old mill stands over by the village. I believe it is used as an observation post by the warden of the reserve. Within its tower years ago on a wild winter's night a marshman called Dick Jettens narrowly missed death as the machinery of the mill raced along driven by an easterly gale that had gathered strength from the open sea and flung itself furiously at the mill. Dick was about to set the sails but a wheel grasped part of his coat and in the near dark he was flung violently against the floor and then, as though he were a rag doll, it flailed him up and down. If he screamed none would have heard for the wind shrieked louder and the nearest cottage, that of old Di Thain, the Broadsman, was half a mile away. Dick was battered into unconsciousness and then when his end was a fibre away, his coat ripped up the back seam and he was flung like a baggage and out of reach of the jaws of the clanking grinding wheels. Afterwards one arm was severely crippled and had to be bound in leather.

Horses on the marshes near West Somerton

Mr Mallett of Kerrison's Level on the Acle Straight, Yarmouth

Mr Mallett manages 700 acres of grazing marsh for Lord Fairhaven and might be caring for as many as 600 head of cattle through the summer months as well as some sheep. He walks or drives around the marshes in a landrover to check the cattle for footrot or wooden tongue, calling in the veterinarian if necessary. Thistles have to be sprayed and in the winter foot drains and dykes are cleared. He has lived with his family at the farm for the past 25 years. He and his wife look so exceedingly well, hearty and contented and are testimonies to the legends of the long-living marsh people hereabouts.

Formed by drainage and reclamation of alluvial land in the valleys, the grazing marshes occupy large areas in the mid and lower reaches of the broadland rivers. Although the grass lands are generally poor botanically, they nevertheless support large populations of birds such as lapwing and snipe, while during the winter they form the favoured feeding ground for wild geese and duck. However it is to the system of drainage of dykes that the naturalist now turns for an insight into what the broads themselves supported before the demise of their aquatic wildlife. Where cattle and horse grazing is still the main form of management, these dykes possess a fabulously rich assemblage of aquatic plants and insects. Water soldier is often so abundant that it can completely cover the water surface. The local dragonfly, the Norfolk Aeshna, has found refuge in these dykes and along with other species of dragonfly and damselfly, all formerly widespread throughout Broadland, can be seen hawking for insects on warm summer days.

overleaf: *Cattle on Kerrison's Level*

Ted Ellis

When I think of Ted Ellis I shall probably always picture one of the most delightful images of men at work I have seen. He sat bathed in the gentle morning sunlight that filtered through a curtained window. In front of him was an old typewriter that may have been the same one he used to type out A.P. Patterson's manuscripts. The oval table it rested on was scattered with books and letters, specimens and paraphernalia. Ted was absorbed in peering at specimens; puffing at his pipe and then, checking a letter, would proceed to type out a reply.

Earlier he had guided me round Wheatfen, aptly described as a paradise of its kind; being comprised of woodland, reedbeds, carr and open water which in this winter was expanded considerably by the high tides.

I felt the same kind of elation in its unspoilt surroundings as I had at Hickling when, running for sheer enjoyment by the reedbeds, I had a Marsh Harrier as pacemaker, and then on the St. Benet marshes during the heatwave of 1976 I had been chased by a herd of bullocks and escaped their attentions only by fleet of foot and a convenient ligger.

What a lovely name for the cottage, Captain Cockle's ... the name of the previous owner who was a great friend and fellow naturalist who died in 1945. Extensions to the cottage have been quickly filled with fascinating piles of books, papers and coypu skulls, fungi and various specimens. My children Susan and Johanna

found the place irresistible. Ted, having shown them round, remarked, 'They use their eyes you see. They look and learn.' whereas Jenny and I sat politely, hesitant to wander. On discovering a new cup fungus he experienced one of the most memorable moments of his life. He had reasoned that there ought to be a seborrhoea living on the catkins of bog myrtles, because there was an ecological gap for it, but it was missing. So he searched and found it. With understandable pride he has said, 'I regard that as a triumph of imagination.' Nowadays we see him on the television often beaming with happiness as memory evokes merriment, and his face

lights up so naturally as he recalls such events as the weird sound of a Bittern's booming throbbing through mist-laden air ... then taking a huge breath Ted performed and emitted a passable 'ooooom himself. He talks so knowledgeably on a wide range of subjects and as stated elsewhere in this book by John Buxton, he possesses wisdom and the ability to work with others peaceably. In spite of numerous visitors and small boys from the village seeking the permission to be 'accounted for' before entering the wilderness, there remains a surprising degree of tolerance for a family so busy as Ted's.

A Dragonfly laying eggs as she skims the surface of the water creating wash with legs and tail

Bluetit feeding young

*Hoisting sail, Pleasure Boat Staithe,
Hickling*

The Broads now comprise some 42
lakes of predominantly freshwater
surrounded by various types of
fenland vegetation. Over the
centuries considerable reclamation
of these fenlands has been carried
out, particularly on the wider
sections of the river valleys, to
produce the characteristic
landscape of grazing marsh criss-
crossed with dykes. Most of the
Broads are situated on the flanks of
the three main rivers, the Waveney,
Yare and Bure and the latter's major
tributaries the Ant and Thurne. They
are shallow, some extremely so, but
their salinity and water regime vary
considerably. They also vary in size
from small ponds to the 120
hectare expanse of Hickling Broad.

Canada geese dropping in

Stewart Linsel, Warden of The Norfolk Naturalist Trust Reserve, Hickling

I had arranged to meet Stewart at ten o'clock at his office on the East side of Hickling Broad. It was a glorious summer's day and after a short delay whilst Stewart resolved a problem of a misdirected lorry load of fence posts, we got on with the drawing. The courtesy, flexibility and encouragement shown by Stewart was afforded me wherever I went, echoing the atmosphere of the area perhaps, within which there is time for the unexpected, time to adjust. For nature is adjusting every fractional second and we, like fools, have made the mistake of designing our lives around stiff patterns that cannot tolerate flexibilities; that demand almost, that everything be cut and dried, pigeonholed.

Robin Harrison

As a schoolboy Robin became fascinated by Breydon, a lifelong intrigue. He disobeyed his parents and paid ½d as pedestrian at Tollgate on the marsh road to Acle and took jamjar, string and bait to fish in the dykes and the wide water.

He was appointed warden of Breydon in 1928 by the Norfolk Naturalists' Trust and in 1969 The Breydon Nature Reserve was formed. He first wrote a column on observations for Eastern Evening News in 1935 under 'Robin' and

A wherry leaving Breydon by the Waveney, with Berney Arms windmill in the background, after a painting by Sir Arnesby Brown.

Wildfowlers.

except for some censoring of weather information during the war has barely missed a handful of weeks. This sense of persistence and loyalty to the job in hand has no doubt helped him when wildfowling, which demands craft, patience and fortitude in sometimes deplorable conditions. Cattle used to be bought in Ireland and then put to graze on the marshes for two years. They were box fed in the winter on barley meal and linseed cake. Drovers then took them off the marshes and on to the tollgate to Norwich and King's Lynn – seven to

eight hundred bullocks each weighing about a ton in one large herd, literally flooding upon the road. Robin remembers times during winter when the marshes alongside Breydon were 'blue' with geese. Wigeon, which once fed in the ronds or pools between the winter and summer walls, are now on the Wash.

Electrical pumps installed in 1948 replaced the less reliable windmills which had probably allowed flooding of marshes on a 'controlled' scale to persist which had the benefit of seemingly improving the

quality of grasses for feeding livestock.

I believe many folk who love the gentle sight of acres of marsh dotted with black and white Friesians will resist the pressures to convert these troublesome plots to growing more food to add to wasteful man-made mountains of excess. The marshes have that ancient feel about them; only a few weeks ago we could see the Waveney at flood tide gently spilling over her banks and adding to the floodwaters that had swamped the marshes at Beccles and Geldeston.

John Buxton, Estate Manager of The National Trust estate at Horsey

There is a constant struggle to keep the Nature Reserve as conservationally safe as possible and this was largely why John's father gave the estate over to The National Trust. It is an area where the birds have priority and human interference is discouraged. Horsey Parish is on or just below sea level.

The Dutch saw the area as agricultural land and viable only with drainage. On some very old maps the area of the Hundred Stream is shown marked in blue and was long ages ago an estuary. John recalled how he had once met a puzzled angler with rods and map looking for water. Horsey Mere is completely surrounded by a wall and the encircling land is drained into the Mere and this in turn is drained over the Hundred Stream seal-off.

In 1938 there was a severe flood. 100 acres about Hall Farm formed an island in the middle of the sea-swamped marsh. Again in 1953 there was flooding but at Horsey the sea was held back by a matter of a few feet. John remarks: 'If it wasn't for a few so-called cranks there would be few reserves of the character of Horsey and others in Broadland available. Beauty is often at its highest point when other people are absent from the scene. Change is the most alarming thing. "Progress" is responsible for pollution of the Broads. If it happens to the extent of something that cannot be reversed, then it is a very bad thing.

'Ted Ellis has an incredible scientific knowledge but has the ability to put such information over in a very ordinary way. He has an uncanny knack of taking the fire out of an argument by sensible suggestions, reasonings etc. Ted has seen in his own lifetime changes taking place in the region over a considerable period which benefit him with prime knowledge.'

I was reminded of the sea when I saw a long net measuring about one hundred by eight feet hanging to dry in the sun between two trees at The Hall. The previous night, John explained, around midnight, his son, a companion and himself had fished from a small boat by moonlight. The sea is a mile away to the East of the hall and I can imagine the thoughts of those who sleep within earshot of its roaring as it pounds at the sand dune walls. In summertime, Horsey Gap is a popular sea-bathing spot but with very limited access.

Lewis Cox

Lewis is a boatyard owner at Barton. There is a lovely corner hereabouts by his yard. Two or three staithes are cluttered with craft of various types. Quietness reigns, enhanced by the sight of silent yachts setting out for the broad. Inside one of the boatsheds an artist, with considerable skill, has painted large portraits of his favourite filmstars of the forties and fifties.

'The Seagull', London, one third scale spritsail barge. A little beauty, moored by Foundry Bridge, Norwich.

Over the past few years we have seen some fine craft including several spritsail barges. One such owned by Ian Houston called 'Raybel' and a second called 'Thalatta' owned by an Education Trust came to Norwich recently. But the unforgettable sight of the Tall Ships race, Yarmouth last year I missed being away on holiday. There are a surprising number of original craft surviving, including our local trading wherry Albion and such delights as the pleasure wherry Olive.

Wildfowler on Breydon North wall

birds between the houseboats and I was relieved when I approached the first. Sure enough I found a Redshank and I think, a Tern lying at the tideline, these being natural, unavoidable things. What appalled me was the wicked litter: literally thousands of jagged broken bottles that had smashed against the wall and become embedded in the black loathsome mud. Pollution filthy, mindless misuse of free-given gifts like this inland sea.

Now, I understand, man wants to place an expensive barrage across the Yare probably near the old swing bridge. Wise people who know the 'balance' of the area are being ignored and the politically-influenced administrators yet again stride ahead in their desire to leave their 'marks' upon the face of the earth. It seems they are screened from a deep love of the land and water and sky for how can they vote to encourage such eventual decline. The marshes are a natural soakaway for the flooding. Admittedly they are a little dangerous; a nuisance but a long-established one. How much more wisely could the million or so pounds be spent on needier causes, for example recovering the damage being wrought on the Broads and rivers by effluent from sewage, etc. This is where The Broads Society is so relevant and I must join them without further ado, for they strive to restrain any uncaring misuse by careful, informed argument.

Having read 'Robin' the previous night I travelled to Yarmouth to see for myself the effect of the arctic conditions on the wildlife of Breydon.

In driving rain I walked inland from Vauxhall Station past the remains of the swing bridge and around the reserve. Shelduck, with their striking orange and black bands on white, nervously fled hundreds of yards ahead of me and flew across to the cold grey tideline ribboning the mudflats. Waders, like children, fluttered and scattered and feeling like a playground attendant I walked on round the wall. Robin had told me where to look for dead

Yacht entering broad.

Eagle Owl

The Eagle Owl is perhaps symbolic
of sightings in the area or of
occasional visitors or the 'hidden'
rare inhabitants which are less well
known due to their shyness or
isolated habitat, such as the Bittern.

Starlings

They flock in huge numbers at dusk during late summer and autumn hurrying across the sky sometimes wheeling and performing aerobatics that the Red Arrows would be proud of, as they head for the reedbeds of broads like Barton and Hickling.

The element of surprise figures largely in broadland bird-watching. At Hickling, for instance, on a shimmering July day, a party of spoonbills may circle down out of the hazel blue sky to alight on the Rush Hills, a favourite haunt of waders. You may happen on a passage visitation of black terns and find them taking their fill of gnats or resting, Andalusian blue in the sunshine, on golden reed stuff. Landing at a river's edge during the holiday month of August, you may see goldfinches lively on the seeding thistles. Winter brings other surprises. Flocks of fieldfares and redwings seek night sanctuary in the sallow bushes and reed grounds after they have been feeding in the uplands during the day. Magpies gather together amongst the alders as night falls. Waxwings come to swallow berries that glow in fiery clusters upon the guelder-rose bushes in the carrs. You may catch a glimpse of a lordly peregrine upon a sentinel tree, or a little merlin flying off with a blackbird almost as big as itself.

Black-tailed godwit.

A Coypu

Two studies of a woodmouse after
Archibald Thorburn

The Coypu, an aquatic mammal superficially resembling a giant rat, was brought to Norfolk from the Argentine in 1929 and bred in captivity for its valuable fur. In 1937 a few of the animals escaped and succeeded in establishing suitable breeding colonies along the river margins. They multiplied and spread quickly to all the broads, which provided them with almost inexhaustible supplies of food in the form of aquatic and marsh vegetation.

Coypus grow to about the size of otters and some specimens have weighed 25 lb. They are dark brown above and lighter beneath and have blunt noses, very large incisor teeth, webbed hind feet and scaly, rat-like tails. The females suckle their young from teats situated high along the sides, both in and out of water. Breeding goes on throughout the year and from two to three litters of from three to eleven young (commonly five) are produced in the course of twelve months. It is usual for a good many to be born in the inclement months of January and February, with the result that in hard winters the offspring are found dead in the marshes where both they and some of the older animals perish through eating frozen vegetables. They are nocturnal feeders and sleep by day on small platforms built in reed beds, in couches gnawed out of sedge-tussocks or at the roots of bushes, or in burrows. A warm summer day will sometimes bring them out to frolic in quiet waters. On such occasions they may be seen floating with their tails stiffly erect, or wallowing for pure pleasure, like hippopotamuses in an East African river. Quiet through the day, at night however, they utter mournful cries at intervals, especially when there is moonlight. It is a weird experience to hear a number of such animals crying through the mist. Because of their nuisance to man they were trapped extensively and their numbers were significantly cut back after 1963.

On the other hand they had contributed to improvements for example by opening water channels which regenerated acres of fen reeds. Some smaller broads had areas of reed bed eaten back thus increasing open water. Mud flats that provided excellent nesting sites for black-headed gulls and common terns; while ducks and waders found them useful feeding places.

Foxes have been known to prey on them but there are very few foxes in the broads district. Young coypus have been found dead with wounds inflicted by stoats, herons and bitterns on occasion. Marsh harriers and owls attack them once in a while; but many other birds, including mallard, moorhens and waterrails, are to be seen feeding amicably with coypus in the swamps.

Curlew and young

Susan and Johanna had joined about twenty other people on the frozen surface of Malthouse Broad. Several men wore skates and moved around a prepared rink of smooth ice fashioned out of the recent snowfall. Overhead geese in small flights flew across to the higher ground. As we gathered the children and left for home I noticed a large flock of geese in a field near The Malsters. With the camera I walked cautiously towards the geese over snow-covered furrows ribboned blue and gold in the dying

Geese on stubble (from a painting by Peter Scott)

sunlight. I felt a fractional part of the cruel joy a wildfowler might experience as he prepares to blast into such a quarry . . . I raised my camera and began an eighteen shot series of colour film recording, the geese nearest to me nervously looking about and then one, playing more safe than the rest, spread great wings and was airborne. Quickly others followed forming a flight and this action ran through the flock so that as I walked on, flight by flight rose into the cold gold air and wheeled toward the broad.

Geese in flight (from a painting by Peter Scott)

The Weasel

The weasel thrives everywhere in the marsh country, where it preys on field voles and moles to a large extent. Birds on the ground are sometimes seized by weasels lurking in mole runs. The animals are extremely secretive and their breeding quarters are seldom discovered. As in the case of stoats, the young are led forth in packs and may be met with on marsh banks occasionally, running with their heads close together, attended by their mother, on a trial hunting expedition. Weasels take to the water readily but are not such regular climbers as stoats. Like the latter they make winter nests in reed stacks, lining them with reed fluff and the fur of moles and voles.

Little Owl

The Little Owl is a fairly common resident, nesting in hollow trees and old buildings. It appears to be more numerous towards the coast, especially in the vicinity of Horsey.

Angry swan and cygnets

The drawing of the parent swan is from a painting by Jan Asselyn I saw in the Rijksmuseum, Holland in 1964.

I am not embarrassed any more by talking about my studying from other artists. It has always existed and is therefore a normal thing especially if accurate attribution of source is given. Having had no master in the flesh I have had to look to the results of their diverse labours and it has been a fascinating, if somewhat unplanned, curriculum. Eventually, I believe, provided the artist resists the temptation to develop into a forger, his own unique qualities will begin to appear. In some cases this may be a rapid process as in the case of Girtin or Bonnington: masterful by their mid-twenties but tragically dying so very young. On the other hand development might be slow but singularly sure, like Constable, who patiently evolved a draughtsmanship and painting manner that pleased two tricky worlds: the artists' and the publics'. What matters is a truly purposeful search for the gift that has been planted in you, but how to illuminate that gift? Like the world at large, art colleges have dived into an experimental pit over recent decades and some of its products have been loathsome but to be fair, there have been some vigorous and

Bewick swan

altogether good works. Not that I know them thoroughly. Mine can only be a sample comment as it were. I believe strongly that we can do much better. We have succumbed to the evils of commercialism and immorality and is it not surprising that our works have mirrored the poverty of our position. One interesting exception, broadly speaking, are The Ruralists whose absorption with the particular is producing interesting

results. If we could strip away some of the dust sheets of haughty establishment-like bewitchery and get down to an honest working relationship with the craft of art on an everyman's basis, this too would help. But there will always be the shallow snob who enjoys his echo chamber and encourages the purchase of stacks of ordinary bricks and piles of sand. May I use my cold water primarily for watercolouring in future.

Canada geese and young

This sketch reminds me of an afternoon at Hoveton Little Broad when Jenny and I with the children had taken a picnic and driven to Don and June Wilson's house, Heron Lodge, Horning, where 'Wendine' was moored. We gingerly set off with our Seagull outboard popping and puffing away. We moved upstream but quickly stalled. Three times the engine failed before a young angler showed me that the airscrew on the petrol cap needed slackening. This like magic, helped the outboard to run like a dream thereafter. The dinghy is low in the water and passing cruisers dwarf her, but it's exciting wondering if you can ride the wash waves successfully. Entering the broad is lovely, past sentinel reed beds and then you see the relatively large open water before you. We headed for a quiet corner, dropped the mud weight and thought of little other than tea. The geese came up so close we fed them by hand and we could see into their deep brown eyes. Idyllic.

Shelduck feeding by the Breydon wall within the reserve area.

44

Heron wading

Mute swans are resident and abundant. Flocking takes place after the nesting season and numbers up to 300 are often present on Hickling Broad. There is numerous evidence that many riverbank landowners in the broadland parishes of Norfolk kept swans under royal licence in the fifteenth and sixteenth centuries, marking their bills with distinctive notches. Few of at least the original 195 or so east Norfolk rights are exercised but cygnets are still caught each summer on the river Yare, marked and pinioned by Norwich City Council.

Little owl with moth

Barn owl

Weasel

A character like this frequently keeps me company on the road to St Benet's abbey. He or she flies from fence post to gatepost. I remember when Jenny's cousin, Jill and her husband Dean, lived out at Brown's Hill by The Ant, as we approached their cottage on occasional visits a barn owl would sometimes float into the air, ghostlike and fascinating.

They nest in derelict mills, local church towers and farm buildings. They are apparently, as my observations have borne out, not uncommon, but are sparsely distributed. It hunts methodically, quartering the marshes not only at dusk but also in broad daylight.

Great crested grebe

The grebe is a summer resident and readily seen on broads and rivers. By Ranworth maltings one afternoon a grebe played a kind of hide and seek with me: it seemed to follow me, and, as I walked around the staithe and the broad, it dived and surfaced keeping nicely distant. Most birds arrive on the broads during February and depart for the estuaries and coastal waters in autumn.

Stock dove

The stock dove is a fairly common resident round the fringes of broadland, often feeding on marshes and in the waterside carrs.

Sedge warbler

An abundant visitor in summertime is the Sedge warbler. It nests chiefly amongst the 'outside' reed-beds close to the water's edge. The fluff from sallow catkins is often worked into the outer fabric of the nest. Examination of illustrations by Thorburn and others or photographs of this particular bird species will show how hard it is to tell them apart unless you are used to spotting vital, subtle differences.

49

Young fox

The fox used to be almost unknown
in the vicinity of the broads and so
far as East Anglia is concerned, it is
almost wholly an introduced
species, put down for hunting. I
don't suppose the 'gentry' could get
a good enough run hereabouts
without getting their boots wet, to
justify a stirrup cup worth the name.

Short-eared owl

A regular autumn passage migrant and a somewhat irregular summer resident in broadland. It has been suggested that the presence or absence of breeding birds and their numbers may depend upon the comparative abundance or scarcity of field voles in the area. Walking along the shores of the Ant recently, I disturbed four adult short-eared owls. They flew off impressively across the marshes. I wondered if I might find anything of their nests, so I searched the area they had fled from. I found no nest but I did find a pellet which is the disgorged bones and fur etc of its victim, in the form of a cylinder tapered at each end and approximately two inches in length.

Bearded tit

The Bearded tit is a rather scarce resident in this area, nesting chiefly in the vicinity of Hickling Broad and Horsey Mere. Wandering flocks visit other broads in winter.

Heron in flight

I completed the drawing of the Old Maltings, Ranworth with the church distant. Afterwards, I decided to walk to the reedbeds east of Malthouse Broad, toward Ward Marsh. The paved road ends by an old farm and the way continues as a dirt road, rutted in the manner of ancient ways, bordered by oak and hawthorn hedges and an occasional holly. Over the gate I could see, sadly, that the old delapidated barn had been burnt down. As I walked closer I could see that apart from the charred oak posts, there were only rusting thatching hooks and brittle, charred reeds lying disordered on the ground. I went along the dyke at the edge of the reed bed and looked across to the church tower and I felt a great sense of timelessness. Hundreds of years could fall away, stimulated by the absence of any contemporary object. (As John Buxton said to me, 'Beauty is often at its highest when no other human being is about.') The sun, very low now, shot countless golden beams across the land and turning to its glistening source, I saw everything gleamed: reeds were silvered; grass was swept with a golden mantle; leaves sparkled and behind me the great reed bed whispered some age-old story, sang some timeless song.

Momentarily time was suspended, cares fell away and I was caught in the warm, transforming sunbeams which seemed to cleanse and drain me of everything save an admiration for my creator God.

I went on and in the distance small flights of cormorant from Breydon and geese from elsewhere were heading for the Ranworth reserve. Then into the sky rose my favourite bird. That mixture of grace and gangling awkwardness, the heron. It ascended two hundred feet and then it began to encircle me. At least, I believed I was its interest. It isolated me with its lofty encirclement, following some invisible perimeter. Then, too soon, it glided away to feast from dyke rich marshes.

Swans taking off

Swans remind me of opposites.
They are at once graceful and
smooth and yet see them begin to
take off and they are the clumsiest
creatures. We human beings
likewise are a strange mixture of
beauty and ugliness . . . especially
within. As a Russian writer declared:
If you cut through the heart of the
greatest saint you would find a
corner of the utmost evil. This little
verse tries to reveal something of
our reluctance to admit the inner
ugliness of our natures. It echoes
too, the piercing force needed to
break into the closely-guarded
inner room of our beings: the sword
of truth. The power of God, by the
living word of Jesus Christ.

Can this clumsy, noisy, flapping
  fiend be really me?
Aren't I that graceful bird on
  whispering wing?
Not you . . . not you, you ugly thing
Why you with flapping feet and
  clammering tongue
Are not in any way worthy of my
  song
What is that I hear you say, my
  brother, you my brother?
Oh brother dear, forgive me; You
  were never near
Until the sword of truth pierced my
  heart and made it clear.

Nightjars

Summer visitors including the
Nightjar can be found in some of
the heaths and woods fringing parts
of broadland.

Bewick swans in flight

The Bewick is a passage migrant
and winter visitor usually in rather
smaller numbers than the whooper.

Common partridges

Kingfisher leaving nest hole

The Kingfisher is resident and fairly common although as in severe winters, subject to serious thinning out of numbers. I have rarely sat with binoculars for the purpose of birdwatching, for I have always wanted to use such opportunity to draw or paint, and so I have never seen such sights as a family of kingfishers gathered on a willow branch but I have occasionally glimpsed the lightning flash of brilliant blue, green and gold as a kingfisher sped from beneath a bridge near St. Benet's or by the waterside of South Walsham Broad.

(overleaf) The beauty of cruising under sail, in harmony with the elements

Scenery

Owen Waters: Painters in Broadland

The landscape of the Broads has inspired many painters. It is because landscape brings the painter closer to the heart of Nature that it arouses in him feelings and moods quite different from those of the portrait or figure painter. In a figure composition characters must be represented with emotions of their own, which the beholder catches and induces in himself by sympathy. This sympathy is of a different kind from the impersonal sympathy prompted by the moods of Nature. These moods are purely subjective, for trees, clouds and rivers do not smile or weep as human characters do.

What is the clue to greatness in painted landscape? If we look back over the whole range we shall, I think, conclude that the most moving paintings are not those in which the topography of a scene is given with truth, nor even with beauty. The really best ones are by men who have responded to the moods of Nature rather than to the visual facts of scenery. Landscape is literally 'the look of the land', it is the physiognomy of the land, its face from which we read all sorts of feelings and signs. The countryman knows intimately the land he cultivates and lives in; he looks up at the sky, which sends light and rain; but the landscape hardly affects him at all unless something has stirred him within to form an image of it. This something, which is the image or picture-making urge: where does it come from, and why? It is more than map-making or making an accurate representation such as a photograph. One could say that a picture is to a map as a poem is to a report. The picture is in a certain sense our own creation; and we seek, if we are urged further, its embodiment in the material world. When we start to paint we find that what we see is conditioned by our ability to reproduce our vision as much as by the means we have of realising it. It makes a great deal of difference whether you see something with a pencil in your hand or without a pencil in your hand. In the last resort we paint only what pleases us. And what pleases us? What we can paint, and finally we see only what corresponds to our sense of beauty.

These general considerations cannot be left out of any account of the art of the region which has individuality of landscape. Firstly, because the 'spirit of the place' is an elusive quality, to be elucidated only through intimate acquaintance and study. Secondly, if the picture-making urge is basically a spiritual one, the art of the region will depend for its ultimate value upon the quality of intention and philosophical vision of its artists. Let us now consider the Broads region in the light of these remarks.

If you draw a circle on a map of Norfolk, taking as centre a point slightly west of Acle and a radius of ten miles, you will encompass roughly the whole area, a small one, in which the dominant features are reed-lined rivers, shallow lakes, marshes, farms and small villages. The marshes, now drained, border the rivers which once flooded and flowed over them to make broad estuaries. Years of systematic drainage and cultivation have tamed the wilderness there once existed, but pockets of it remain. Since water at the lowest level dominates the landscape, the horizon is a long level one, the sky is tremendous and the light very strong. Nearness to the sea and complete openness to the elements ensures a landscape whose colour and tone are constantly changing and are seldom monotonous. The weather is an important arbiter of beauty in landscape, and it shows itself in paintings as varying conditions of light and atmosphere. I guess that the artistic appreciation of landscape and the painting of it derived largely from townsmen's holidays in the country when journeys were serious undertakings. Nature appreciation at first was for the wealthy, who could travel abroad, chiefly to Switzerland and Italy. By degrees, the 'scenery' idea trickled through to the middle classes who found what they wanted in the British Isles. Only a few painters were inspired by Nature's moods and effects, apart from her forms, and it was perhaps Constable who first drew attention to them in his work. Through him landscape began to exert a fascination, independant of the grand forms popularised by Claude, Wilson and Turner. Constable painted most of his pictures within a few square miles of his East Anglian home. Artists now felt that unexpected beauties lurk in ordinary, homely scenes, all seen under some passing aspect of what we may call weather. And from that time onward landscape painting of the best kind concerned itself with problems of beauty as brought about by light and air. How did this process work in East Norfolk? The so-called Norwich School painters had the right attitude. In the Oxford Companion to Art, their work is described as 'unpretentiously

provincial and unconcerned to rival the réclame of official art'. And it has been said that English landscape painting was in origin 'a form of modest self-expression by provincials, a record by simple men of their own happiness in their fields and villages'. This is no doubt true, but there were one or two great painters among them who could lift the homely charms of our local scenery to the heights of great art. I refer to John Crome and Henry Bright.

There are two outstanding requirements for the convincing presentation of landscape: a sense of space, and homogeneity or 'oneness'. These qualities belong to any actual view and are therefore basic. Let's examine them briefly.

It's a fact that if in a landscape picture we see objects incorrectly or clumsily drawn, their faults will be largely condoned if their tones are correctly graded to keep them in their proper places in space. Unless the painter preserves this correct gradation of tones (called: 'aerial perspective') there will be no 'recession of planes' and therefore no impression of space. The other quality of 'one-ness' is the general look of a scene to which all objects and all parts are contributive, details which, singularly, do not impose themselves in a discordant manner. This is attained by breadth of treatment or handling of the pictorial medium. When such treatment is arrived at, largeness of style results.

This breadth or generalisation becomes the chief delight of the mature painter. At last he looks beyond the variety of things Nature offers and finds another aspect of things which gives him greater satisfaction. He does not regard the objects separately but the whole thing, the entity they compose between them. He now looks not analytically but synthetically, and to look in this way requires a special sort of vision that comes with practice. Such a practice and such a vision seizes the individuality of a landscape, its spirit, whilst rendering its separate parts by suggestion. The picture is then more potent to exercise the imagination; it becomes a better medium to convey the feelings of the artist and to engage those of the beholder than it would be if every detail were carefully rendered, thereby keeping the imagination unstirred.

If one looks at Crome's work this largeness and breadth of vision is most striking, and one sees that he towers over the other Norwich School painters. In his best pictures he goes for the great ensemble that is the spirit of the landscape. In his apparently simple statements one sees inexhaustible suggestions of the variety, accidentals, lights, shades and modulations of colour seen in Nature. His 'Moonrise on the Yare' (see page 78) with its monumental stillness and serenity of the silhouetted barns, windmills and boats is the father and mother, the perfect model of all subsequent Broadland painting, that is, painting which looks for the true beauty of the place, but so seldom captures it. In my view there have been, since Crome and his brilliant successor Henry Bright, only three painters whose efforts have succeeded in this area. These three stand out from a host of skilled yet mainly uninspired painters. They were Sir Arnesby Brown, his pupil C.A. Mellon and Edward Seago, and I consider myself fortunate to have met, talked and (in the case of Mellon and Seago) worked with them and to have perceived that their attitude to beauty was rather one of affection than of a keen almost scientific research into its nature. Their grasp of the fact that light is the predominant source of beauty in nature was not scientific but instinctive, and like their great ancestors, Crome and Constable, their sympathy went out to the beauty of the panoramic scene. Panorama, with its suggestion of space and distance, is the essence of flat landscape,and those three recent painters give to our lowly unspectacular countryside almost ethical qualities of dignity and power conveyed excitingly through the accidents of the light in which they saw it. 'Trifles in nature must be overlooked,' said John Crome. I think this means 'over-looked' not 'considered and rejected', which is what we do when we make our pictures, selecting and eliminating from a host of objects seen in nature. Not merely the task of picture-making, but the far more difficult task of picture-seeing. Seago particularly recommended and stressed the importance of this power instead of the conscious process of selection which is a mental process; the power not to see those things in the actual scene which stand in the way of the free exercise of that aesthetic faculty which is an intuitive process. 'Not knowing how or why we are so charmed' was Crome's way of putting it.

It's this gift of instantaneous vision which is the secret of the breadth of Crome, Bright and our three later Norfolk painters. To them, and to those who see as they do, the delight of the eye lies in the very act of seeing. So strong is the force of this delight that when one has caught the sensation of seeing Nature as they did, as an indivisible 'unit of beauty', one often imagines that the actual clouds one sees moving across our Norfolk landscape were designed by them. Of the recent three, there was doubt as to who was the greatest: the other two always acknowledged (to me anyway) Arnesby Brown as the master. In all his art there is no melancholy. Even when there is awe, it is always mixed with the delight of the eye. Peace is its chief note, the peace of contemplation. There is little action, in the use of figures; the only living thing is the light.

On meeting these great painters, I was astonished to find that their landscapes were painted in the studio. This was an impossible process to me who had not learned his Nature through long years of devoted observation. The young and inexperienced cannot do it. Their place is in the open learning. All the fine Norfolk landscapes I admired for their poetry, feeling and truth were studio-made. Many were invented from the imagination, many from mere notes and ideas sketchily recorded. Gradually I came to recognise that their success in capturing in paint the truth of our landscape lay in their devotion to it; to their love of its ever-changing light shining in a majestic space which has a logic of its own, a kind of visual symphony in which all the parts perform together to make a whole, a unified effect greater than the sum of its parts.

It was for these reasons that to the eye of the inexperienced their works appear almost as half-statements, too generalised, too simple. Where the inexperienced sees a landscape teeming with small objects or spots of colour, these artists show no such intricacy but simple statements of a few broad facts of form and colour. And when the art of painting does this, we have as much right to call it poetry as we have to call Wordsworth's verses pictures when they stir us to recollect the things we love in Nature. It is for this quality that Broadland, expressed in the paintings of these perceptive artists, appeals so strongly, not only to natives but to visitors also. Its poetry – I can find no more suitable word – is like an aroma rather than a visual image; it is a repercussion in our deeper sensibilities.

I took Susie and little Jo to the South Walsham marshes one Sunday afternoon recently. At the end of the marsh road we left the car and proceeded up the rutted track towards the Bure. The girls jumped onto every frozen puddle in the ruts they found and had a smashing time. With their wool, bobbled hats they looked like playful pixies and we had quite a laugh when a military-looking gent called to his hound, 'Susie, come here.' Well, our Susie curled up against her sister and they both endeavoured to avoid the attentions of the over-friendly dog. Reaching the Bure and heading for Thurne Mouth we saw the river frozen in wide strips of glistening ice either side. Here and there the river had spilled over the bank and these ponds were likewise ice-surfaced. The light was beautiful.

The colour scarce with occasional gold reeds accenting the overall nuances of blues that danced upon the surface of the land but with a delicate wash of warm gold overlaying the whole. Immediately, I remembered the traffic of the summer and knew what a treasure a time such as this represented. Perhaps the St. Benet founders first saw the Bure like this?

A tragic tinge to the afternoon was the sighting of a Bewick swimming on the other side of the river with a badly broken wing trailing in the water. Susie called and called to it, in the most entreating manner, but the luckless bird swam into 'safety' behind the far ice flow, refusing to be rescued. With some tears Susie joined Jo and I, and we headed homewards as the mists of evening began to descend upon the empty marshes.

Young man resting on river bank.

Even on nature reserves control over water quality and recreational boating pressure is largely impossible to achieve as responsibility for these functions are vested in different authorities. In an attempt to resolve these conflicts of interests, the Countryside Commission initiated in 1976 consultations on the possibility of establishing a National Park for the Broads. Although not an ideal solution the Nature Conservancy Council believes that with a suitable amending legislation a National Park could go a long way to solving many of the administrative and management problems that currently bedevil Broadland. Without a National Park or special Broadland Authority the biological heritage of this national asset will decline to the point where recovery will not be technically or economically feasible.

More recently efforts have been made to appoint a Broadland Commissioner to coordinate overall control, but so far, with some mystery, the successful candidates have declined to take up the post at the last minute.

River Waveney at Beccles.

Berney Arms windmill through the reeds

Sailing by mill at Thurne Mouth

This windmill was restored under the ownership of Norwich Union Life Insurance Society by millwrights, Lennard and Lawn in 1973. The sails will usually turn in a strong wind as the brake is usually left free. It is maintained at the above Society's expense by Mr. Richard Seago. With its companion, the white painted Thurne dyke mill, it forms a particularly unique sight, whether from the river or anywhere about the marshes or above Thurne village by the old church. They are the only two restored windpumps standing in close proximity to one another on any waterway in this country.

Angler in the isolation of some quiet corner of a broad.

St. Olaves on the Waveney

River at eveningtime

In the evening the noise of the day subsides. The rivers take on an air of solitude and peace and perhaps a few, just a precious few, yachts patiently tack from bank to bank, withdrawing the hushed power of the cool summer breeze.

Moored cruisers on a broad

Cattle at Browns' Hill on the River Ant

Thankfully, there are still many quiet roads in broadland where traffic is minimal and you can be forgiven for dreaming that those years you have experienced are but a moment; that you are walking as a child remembering similarly quiet, marvellously peaceful ways.

Sailing across the mouth of Fleet Dyke by St. Benet's Abbey

At above five o'clock in the afternoon I went off to South Walsham marshes to get a breath of fresh air and to see if there was anything of interest about. I had to sketch and photograph some willows that I knew grew in three or four clumps along the dyke.

I parked the car by the private yacht basin and scampered off walking as fast as I could, for I was hoping to get back early evening for supper. Initially the going was good, but the old path seemed to have been lost and a new one nearer the bank of the dyke established by anglers. About half way along it became overgrown and ill-defined and I was almost blindly struggling along feeling through my shoes for the depression of the original path farther from the bank. But due to the heavy, prolonged rain through summer, the reeds, nettles, brambles and wildflowers had grown tremendously high and thick, making progress very difficult.

My shoelaces were pulled undone; my clothes were decorated with sticky burrs and bramble thorns and my legs began to irritate with repeated nettle stings. I had the bit between my teeth by this time and as I was getting one or two lovely shots of trees in sparkling light, I decided to keep going.

I came upon a cruiser in which an old lady languished somewhat awkwardly in the stern, whilst her husband fished nearby. I searched round and spotted a good subject, became preoccupied with it and promptly let go of my sketchpad which slipped from beneath my arm and fell with a quietish plop into the dyke. I bent down, embarrased, and quickly retrieved my book and then proceeded to disappear into the nearby reeds, clicking my camera as I went. Well, this old lady looked ever so oddly at me as I went. I struggled on, congratulating myself on my progress and the fact that I had kept my shoes dry. I negotiated the roots around a large willow, took one or two shots within the curtained enclosure of its trailing branches and then struck on into a jungle of high, dense reeds and weeds.

Fairly close to quitting, I looked eastwards across the South Walsham marshes and saw the unmistakable large single sail of a wherry . . . shining white and moving majestically up river on the Bure from Thurne Mouth.

This justified all discomfort and gave me cause to rush on like a pheasant startled by a stout gun-carrying farmer. I fell over at one point, stopped to pull my shoe on and secure the lace; muttered at my reasoning but was cheered by the occasional sight through the reeds of the fast converging wherry. I was hopping along heading for St. Benet's . . . I nearly leapt out of my shoes as a covey of partridge broke cover with their explosive wing beat. I thought they had all fled when another rose and caused my heart to race as it burst away in a sudden shattering of the quiet.

Finally I emerged at the end of Fleet Dyke, snapping as I went at the wherry, much to the intrigue of three cruisers tied up nearby.

'There's a wherry coming along, well worth a look,' I said to a young man in glasses, who promptly got his camera and ran after me.

We proceeded to the very edge of the bank across a low height reed bed and waited for the vessel to appear.

A yacht, sails bulging with wind approached and I recognised a local bishop who looked puzzled when I called, 'Hello' but answered with a smile as he steered skillfully close to the river's edge.

Then the wherry came in sight. She was a pleasure wherry and a rare beauty, glistening and gleaming in her varnished finery

and carrying with due pride a sail of white that gathered a generous supply of the wind about. At first it looked as though she might be mooring over against the St. Benet's bank but apparently the skipper knew of the rotten, dangerous, submerged piles there for the 'Olive' sailed on and the sight of her was worth every struggling step I had taken. I was going snap, carefully snap – saving a precious few frames for when she drew level against the backdrop of the ruined gateway. She grew bigger and bigger, rising grandly above the surroundings like a giant queen in bright raiment – shining, sparkling as sweet a sight as I've seen. Then she was past. Her crew smiled at the interest. Too soon she was away, her two tenders roller-coasting her wash and her red ensign waving a farewell.

'Could you give me a lift up the dyke. Have you had tea?' I asked the young man with glasses.

'Yes. I think we could and no we haven't,' he answered.

As we returned to his boat, a bathtub cruiser with four young crew aboard swung into the dyke.

'I'll try to get a lift off them. It'll save you the trouble,' I said. We were walking by the bank and as I looked across and called to the bathtub. 'Can you give me a lift please?' This was answered with three blank stares and one tentative reply, 'We no speak English.'

So I stuck my thumb in the air and rapidly gesticulated with it towards South Walsham Broad but as I did so my right leg plunged into the dyke up to my kneecap as I succeeded in finding a hole in the bank where erosion had defeated the piling. With a weak smile I

recovered my leg and thought, 'What must these people think of me – having emerged from the reed jungle, panting and puffing, snapping and clicking, gesticulating across the marshes and muttering, "wherry, wherry!" Now this . . . they must have considered they had bumped into a nitwit or something.' 'Don't worry,' the young man with glasses said, 'I'll take you down', as I tried gesturing to a second cruiser whose occupants pointed to the adjacent moorings.

Well we set off without mishap and enjoyed a short run past the jungle whereupon the young man with seasonal inexpertise gave his boat a severe hull-ache as he rammed the wooden piles at modest speed, sharp-end on. I leapt ashore, dryly, turned and waved a grateful goodbye.

Fleet dyke, (Disaster Cut as far as I am concerned) with St. Benet's Abbey in the distance.

Reeds, reeds . . . there are regiments of them. They stand and wave like children lining a royal route, gathered gracefully at the waterside and the wind passes along their ranks and they dip and bow most gracefully. Or, as in the massive beds off the rivers where the gentlest breeze seems to cause within their thousands, a response as of a giant hushed voice that whispers all around. How strange, how indescribably lovely it is to stand and listen to the sighing of the wind through the reeds.

But these beautiful plants that are so perfectly suited to defend the waterways have been given little chance of survival because of man's stupidity. They are destroyed by disturbance and other factors and in their place what do we see . . . stark, stiff piling that is expensive and doomed to corrosion and rot.

Reedbed at the edge of a broad

69

Sailing cruisers by Ludham Bridge

Broadland as elsewhere has experienced change but there are still places that, at the right moment, in the absence of such sounds as heavy road traffic and too many river craft, could conceivably cause you to believe you have been transported back in time to decades ago. Times when the earlier holidaymakers found this area a paradise: clear, pure waters clothed with lilies and rich with plant life, fish and fowl. The loss of aquatic plant life is due mainly to the over-enrichment of the waters by treated sewage effluent and artificial fertilizers washed out from the surrounding farmland.

Racing at Horning

Sailing cruisers during the 1977 Yare Navigation Race. The area has many regattas and races, including the recently revived Acle Regatta; and this beautiful race illustrated that sets off from Coldham Hall.

(overleaf) *Shooting Acle Bridge and travelling up the Bure to Thurne*

The Present Day

The establishment of 899 hectares as nature reserves by the Nature Conservancy Council, Norfolk Naturalist's Trust, Royal Society for the Protection of Birds and National Trust has enabled conservationists to safeguard part of Broadland's wildlife. By ensuring the continuation of traditional management practices such as reed and sedge harvesting, conditions are maintained for species favouring open fen. Similarly, treatment centres established during periods when botulism is rife save at least some of the toxin-poisoned birds. Visitors are encouraged to appreciate Broadland's wildlife through the provisions of facilities such as nature trails established by the Nature Conservancy Council at Hoveton Great Broad and by the Norfolk Naturalist's Trust at the Ranworth Conservation Centre and also at Hickling Broad. Bird watching hides are also available at several reserves including Hickling Broad and the Royal Society for the Protection of Birds' reserve at Strumshaw Fen.

View from the top of Ranworth Church tower

The climb up the worn spiral stone steps is well rewarded by the unparalleled view across to Thurne and Ludham.

The church interior offers coolness; great beauty of simple design; a rood screen and a fascinating ancient book hand written and illustrated.

The peaceful sight of anglers and sails

I left the inner-city traffic with its vicious noise, puntuated at times by those ghoulish sirens and forgot the smells and the unlovely sights and sounds as I sped into the country down the quiet Salhouse Road out of Norwich.

Reaching Malthouse Broad on a mellow autumn afternoon I found it sleepy and peaceful. There were several cruisers and yachts by the quay and bell-weighted on the open water. There was an air of tranquility about, helped by the stillness of the air; people moved leisurely about; sailing vessels passed to and fro and a large triangular mainsail hung limply at its mast as the crew enjoyed a late lunch.

The sunlight was gentle and enriching, colouring the world in deep and golden hues. The broads surface was rippled by the moving yachts and by coots, grebes and a variety of duck and they, together with the sky and the sails, made a fascinating ever-changing picture that mesmerised two anglers fishing by a clump of Alder as well as others who had time to stand and stare idly by.

I sketched little coots and their restless, rippling reflections, yachts as they moved gracefully to moorings. A generous, retired man from Dereham offered to take me to wherever I wished to sketch from but I thanked him warmly, and replied that I was very happy as I was.

There was an air of contentment and goodwill about the place.

Ranworth Maltings with the church in the background

75

Yachts on Fleet Dyke

One blisteringly hot day in the heatwave summer of 1976, I took my canoe to Malthouse Broad in order to paddle up Fleet Dyke to sketch St. Benet's. On the way back in the early afternoon I found the desire to drowse irresistible and I remember trying to warn myself not to dose off. But too late I was away and spinning, falling and with a great splash I was over and upside down in the water before I could shout help. Fortunately, I struggled out of the cockpit and swam the few yards to the bank. Eventually I presented myself back home to Jenny, dressed only in my purple underpants and smelling like a sewer.

*Coldham Hall on the River Yare: a
beautiful area of wide-spanning
interest*

Water in picturesque surroundings
always attracts visitors and the calm
beauty of the Broads has provided
enjoyment for holidaymakers for
almost a hundred years. Today it
supports a nationally important
tourist industry with some 2,040
hire boats and 7,570 private boats
licensed to use the 200 kilometres
of navigable waterways. Anglers
can still find good coarse fishing
although the fabled pike fishing of
pre-war years is now a thing of the
past. For the naturalist, the
patchwork of open water,
reedswamp, fen and scrub
woodland is of enormous interest
as it provides the basis for an
amazing variety of plant and
animals; some of these are national
varieties.

*Sailing by Coldham Hall, crewman
using a trapeze*

Yare Navigation Race

A police launch. Extremely smart and a credit to the force.

John Crome's, 'Moonrise on the Yare'.

Said to be Berney Arms with Burgh Castle in the background to the right. In my study from this work I have emphasised the castle bastions. (See page 60 and 61, Owen Waters, 'Painters in Broadland'.)

Ducks getting up from a broad

Psalm 8

1 Lord our Lord, how excellent is thy name in all the earth! who hast set thy glory above the heavens.

2 Out of the mouth of babes and sucklings hast thou ordained strength because of thine enemies, that thou mightest still the enemy and the avenger.

3 When I consider thy heavens, the work of thy fingers, the moon and stars, which thou hast ordained;

4 What is man, that thou art mindful of him? And the son of man, that thou visitest him?

5 For thou hast made him a little lower than the angels, and hast crowned him with glory and honour.

6 Thou madest him to have dominion over the works of thy hands; thou hast put all things under his feet:

7 All sheep and oxen, yea, and the beasts of the field;

8 The fowl of the air, and the fish of the sea, and whatsoever passeth through the paths of the seas.

9 O Lord our Lord, how excellent is thy name in all the earth.

Sailing cruiser